AF489222

Goodbye Joe, GOODBYE!

Thomas Paine Jr.

Goodbye Joe, Goodbye!

Thomas Paine Jr.

Copyright2024/Thomas Paine Jr
All Rights Reserved
ISBN: 9798869355973
Proudly Printed In The USA

Goodbye Joe,
GOODBYE!
Thomas Paine Jr.

Goodbye Joe!
You have to go!

Your time here is now through!

We the People
have had enough.

We are sick and tired of you.

We just want to raise
our families

and live out the
American dream.

We don't want another witch hunt
or another one of your schemes.

Your wasteful and needless spending
has left our economy a wreck.

It started when you bought your votes.
In the form of a stimulus check.

Now many working families
can no longer afford to pay their bills.

Thanks to you and all of the others
that sit up there on Capitol Hill.

You sold out
we the people.
You made our border gates
open wide.

More thugs with drugs
now run our streets.
There's nowhere left to hide.

You are a disgrace to your voters.

You are a traitor and a liar.

Just one more thing
before you go.

Hey Sleepy Joe,
You're
FIRED!

www.ingramcontent.com/pod-product-compliance
Lightning Source LLC
Chambersburg PA
CBHW080948130726
48003CB00010BB/3133